**PATHWAY BIBLE GUIDES**

# Standing Firm
## 1 THESSALONIANS

### BY SIMON ROBERTS

*Standing Firm*
*Pathway Bible Guides: 1 Thessalonians*
© Matthias Media 2006


Matthias Media
(St Matthias Press Ltd. ACN 067 558 365)
Email: info@matthiasmedia.com.au
Internet: www.matthiasmedia.com.au
Please visit our website for current postal and telephone contact information.

Matthias Media (USA)
Email: sales@matthiasmedia.com
Internet: www.matthiasmedia.com
Please visit our website for current postal and telephone contact information.

ISBN 978 1 921068 19 5

Cover design and typesetting by Lankshear Design.

# CONTENTS

# BEFORE YOU BEGIN

Wherever the apostle Paul went, he seemed to get into trouble. He was beaten and thrown into jail in Philippi, mocked in Athens, brought before the authorities in Corinth, and forced to leave Thessalonica only a few weeks after his arrival. Of course, none of this was the result of bad behaviour. It was because he continued to preach the message about Jesus Christ.

The gospel is that kind of message. It provokes strong reactions. Some will reject it and work to silence those who speak it. Others will accept it and change because of it.

Some of the Thessalonians had done just this. They had "turned to God from idols to serve the living and true God, and to wait for his Son from heaven" (1:9-10). They had made a great start to the Christian life! But having been driven from the city, Paul was unable to care for these new converts as he would have wanted. So he sent Timothy to visit them and, upon Timothy's return, Paul, Timothy and Silvanus wrote the letter we know as 1 Thessalonians. They wanted to encourage the Thessalonian Christians, and to urge them to *stand firm* in the faith (3:8), even in the face of the opposition they continued to encounter.

*Standing Firm* is a vital aspect of the Christian life. It means sticking with Jesus, come what may. It means continually returning to the message of the cross and the hope of salvation we have through our Lord

Jesus Christ. But as you read 1 Thessalonians, you'll see that it doesn't mean standing still, because Paul's great desire is that "as you received from us how you ought to live and to please God, just as you are doing, that you do so more and more" (4:1). He wants them, and us, to be continually increasing and abounding in love, faith, hope, joy and thanksgiving. And to make sure it's clear what this means in practice, Paul keeps reminding the Thessalonians of the example he set among them.

You may have been a Christian for a long time; or, like the Thessalonians, for only a few weeks. In either case, my prayer is that, having turned to Christ, you will stand firm in him.

*Simon Roberts*
January 2006

# 1. GENUINE IMITATIONS

## 1 Thessalonians 1:1-10

 **Getting started**

Who do you admire so much that you would go so far as to imitate them? What makes that person worth imitating?

## 💡 Light from the Word

Read 1 Thessalonians 1:1-10.

1. How does Paul know that the Thessalonian Christians are loved by God and have been chosen by him (vv. 4-5)?

2. What do you think Paul means when he says the gospel message came to them "not only in word, but also in power and in the Holy Spirit and with full conviction" (v. 5)?

3. What does verse 10 tell us about Jesus and the content of this gospel message?

4. What is the proper way to respond to this news (vv. 9-10)?

5. What changes did the gospel produce in the Thessalonians?

6. In verses 6-8 Paul, Silvanus and Timothy recall how the Thessalonians "became imitators of us and of the Lord", so that they in turn "became an example to all the believers in Macedonia and Achaia". What actions made them imitators and examples?

7. How could the Thessalonians have received the gospel message with joy if they received it in the midst of much affliction (suffering)?

8. Why is the gospel of Jesus a message worth receiving and telling?

 ## To finish

This passage makes it clear that God's gospel can change lives. What things ought you to change, so you can better imitate the example set by the Thessalonians?

 ## Give thanks and pray

- If you are waiting for the return of Jesus and deliverance from the wrath to come, thank God that he has chosen you.
- Ask God to help you better imitate the example of the Thessalonians.

# 2. WALK WORTHILY

## 1 Thessalonians 2:1-12

 **Getting started**

What do you think when people say one thing with their mouths, but a completely different thing with their actions? What does this tell you about the things they say?

## 💡 Light from the Word

Read 1 Thessalonians 2:1-12.

1. In Philippi, Paul had been severely beaten and thrown into jail. In Thessalonica he also encountered strong opposition. Why did Paul continue to declare such an unpopular message (vv. 2-4)?

2. List the motives and tricks which were *not* found in Paul's gospel preaching (vv. 3-6).

3. As an apostle of Christ, Paul could have made demands of the Thessalonians, but he did not want to be a burden on them.

   a. Why did he not want to be a burden (vv. 7-10)?

   b. What did he and his fellow workers do to make sure they weren't a burden (v. 9)?

   c. How is this a demonstration of their deep affection for the Thessalonians (v. 8)?

4. Paul exhorted, encouraged and charged the Thessalonians to "walk in a manner worthy of God" (v. 12). What had he, Silvanus and Timothy done to demonstrate what this kind of life looks like?

5. How would you explain to someone the reason why it is so important for Christians to live holy, righteous and blameless lives (vv. 4, 12, 1:7-10)?

##  To finish

What things can you do to better walk in a manner worthy of God?

##  Give thanks and pray

- Thank God for Paul's example of 'worthy walking'.
- Pray that God would help you to walk in a manner worthy of the kingdom and glory into which you are called.

# 3. THE WORD AT WORK

## 1 Thessalonians 2:13-16

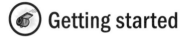 **Getting started**

When was the last time you saw God at work in the world?

# 💡 Light from the Word

Read 1 Thessalonians 2:13-16.

1. What did the Thessalonians hear from Paul, Silvanus and Timothy (v. 13)?



2. The Thessalonians accepted this:

   a. not as _____

   b. but as _____.

3. How can we hear the word of God today?




4. What do you think Paul means when he says the word of God is "at work in you believers" (v. 13)?

5. In verses 14-16:

    a. Why is Paul so negative about "the Jews"?

    b. Is he talking about *all* Jews? Explain your answer. (See also Acts 17:1-4.)

6. What two responses do people have to the word of God? What are the consequences of each response?

7. Why is it so important that we recognize the word of God for what it really is?

 ## To finish

Discuss ways in which you can give the word of God lots of opportunity to work in your life and the lives of others. Compile a group list and then choose one particular way and make it the focus of your prayer time.

 ## Give thanks and pray

- Thank God that he is at work in our lives through his powerful word.
- Pray that you would have opportunities to help this word be at work in the lives of others.

# 4. GOSPEL PRIORITIES

## 1 Thessalonians 2:17-3:13

 **Getting started**

List, in order of importance, three things you would really like to achieve in the next two years. Explain why you put them in this particular order.

## 💡 Light from the Word

Read 1 Thessalonians 2:17-3:13.

1. Why is Paul so eager to see the Thessalonians face to face?

2. Why are we "destined" to suffer affliction (3:3-4)? (Also read John 15:18-21.)

3. Paul was unable to see the Thessalonians in person, so he sent Timothy instead.

   a. What news has Timothy returned with (3:6)?

   b. What is Paul's response to this news (3:7-10)?

4. In 3:11-13, Paul prays that the Lord would:
   - make the Thessalonians "increase and abound in love for one another and for all"
   - establish their hearts "blameless in holiness before our God and Father, at the coming of our Lord Jesus".

   a. What do you think love is? Why is it so important?

   b. What do you think holiness is? Why is it so important?

5. How do these goals that Paul has for the Thessalonians compare with your own goals for your life? (Refer back to the 'Getting started' question on page 19.)

6. What is God's role in bringing about love and holiness in our lives? What is our role?

 ## To finish

Come up with three ways in which you can imitate, in your church context, Paul's deep concern for others.

 ## Give thanks and pray

- Thank God that he is at work in our lives to make us holy.
- Pray that God would help you to act in love and holiness in all situations.

# 5. GOD'S WILL, YOUR SANCTIFICATION

1 Thessalonians 4:1-12

 **Getting started**

People often say that Christians are just hypocrites. Is this true? Should this be true?

# 🔆 Light from the Word

Read 1 Thessalonians 4:1-12.

1.  In verse 1, what is it that Paul asks and urges the Thessalonians to do?




2.  Paul puts this another way in the first half of verse 3:

    a.  He says the will of God for them is their _____.

    b.  What do you think this means in practice?




3.  How are Christians *not* to use their bodies and sexual desires?

4. How *are* Christians to use their bodies and sexual desires?

5. What motives or reasons does Paul provide (vv. 6-8)?

6. Something else Paul wants the Thessalonians to do "more and more" is love one another (vv. 9-10). What kind of "love" do you think Paul has in mind in verses 9-12, and what does it involve?

7. Why are things like quiet living, taking care of your own affairs and working, examples of this kind of love?

8. In 2:11-12 Paul reminds the Thessalonians of how he exhorted, encouraged and charged them to "walk in a manner worthy of God, who calls you into his own kingdom and glory". Here in 4:12, Paul wants them to "live [literally, 'walk'] properly before outsiders". Why are our actions so important?

 ## To finish

As we have seen, living to please God will affect every aspect of our relationships with others. Pick one part of your life where you know you can do more to please God. Then talk about what things you can do to be more loving and holy in this area.

 ## Give thanks and pray

This passage follows on from the prayer in 3:11-13. So you could:
- thank God that he is at work in our lives to make us holy
- pray that God would help you to be self-controlled and to act in love towards all people.

# 6. HOPE IN THE LORD

## 1 Thessalonians 4:13-18

 **Getting started**

Have you ever been to a funeral? Did you feel you had anything helpful to say to those who were most affected by the person's death?

## 💡 Light from the Word

Read 1 Thessalonians 4:13-18.

1. Paul does not want the Thessalonians to be "uninformed... about those who are asleep" (v. 13). What do you think Paul means here by the word "asleep"?

2. Why does he want them to be informed?

3. According to Paul, what is the Christian hope (v. 14)?

4. How do we know this hope is sure and certain, and not just wishful thinking?

5. Will those asleep in Christ miss out in any way when the Lord returns? Explain.

6. Will anyone fail to recognize the coming of the Lord when it happens? Why?

7. What common destiny do those "who have fallen asleep" and those "who are left" share (v. 17)?

8. Paul expects that this hope will change our grief. How do you think it makes a difference?

 ## To finish

In verse 18 Paul concludes by instructing the Thessalonians to "encourage one another with these words". How can you do this?

 ## Give thanks and pray

- Thank God for the hope he has given us in Christ.
- Pray for wisdom as you seek to encourage and comfort others as they grieve.

# 7. READY FOR HIS RETURN

## 1 Thessalonians 5:1-11

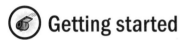 **Getting started**

Think back to a big event in your life (e.g. final exams, the first day of a new job, a wedding). What did you have to do to get ready for that event?

## 💡 Light from the Word

Read 1 Thessalonians 5:1-11.

1. How will the day of the Lord come (vv. 1-3)?

2. Why should Christians not be surprised by this day (vv. 4-5)?

3. Paul says that Christians should "not sleep, as others do, but let us keep awake and be sober" (v. 6).

   a. What do you think Paul means here by the word "sleep"? Is this different to the way he used the word in 4:13-18?

b.  What do you think he means when he says we are to "keep awake and be sober" ("alert and self-controlled", NIV)?

4.  Why is being "awake" and "sober" the only appropriate way of life for Christians?

5.  One way we can be sober is to "put on the breastplate of faith and love, and for a helmet the hope of salvation" (v. 8).

   a.  What is the essence of the Christian faith and hope of salvation (vv. 9-10)?

b. Why do you think we needed Christ to die for us? How does *his* death help *us*?

c. How do you think faith, love and hope can be like armour and help us to be "sober"?

 ## To finish

In verse 11, Paul concludes by instructing the Thessalonians to "encourage one another and build one another up". What are some practical ways you can be helping each other be "awake and sober", ready for the Lord's return?

 ## Give thanks and pray

- Thank God that he has "not destined us for wrath, but to obtain salvation through our Lord Jesus Christ" (v. 9).
- Pray that he would help you to be awake and sober, ready for that day.

# 8. A GOSPEL CHURCH AT WORK

1 Thessalonians 5:12-28

 **Getting started**

When you think of 'church', what comes to mind? What sorts of things do you think 'the church' should be doing?

## ☀ Light from the Word

This letter has been written to "the church of the Thessalonians" (1:1)—that is, to the gathering of Thessalonian Christians. That's what church is: a group of Christians who get together because of what Christ has done for them. But what should church life look like?

Read 1 Thessalonians 5:12-28.

1.  In 5:12-13, Paul speaks about the place of leadership in the church.

    a.  According to Paul, what is Christian leadership about?

    b.  How are we to respond to this sort of loving service? Why?

2.  What other instructions does Paul give in verses 13-15?

    a.  Be at _____.

    b.  _____ the idle.

    c.  _____ the fainthearted (or 'timid').

    d.  _____ the weak.

e. _____ with them all (or 'everyone').

f. See to it/Make sure that _____.

g. But always _____.

h. Who should be doing all these things?

i. How can people be doing all these things, and be so involved with each other's lives, and yet still "be at peace" with each other?

3. Paul also says that God's will for the Thessalonians is that they "rejoice always, pray without ceasing, give thanks in all circumstances" (vv. 16-18).

a. What reason do they have for being so full of joy and thanksgiving? (See also vv. 9-10.)

b. Why do you think being joyful, prayerful and thankful are such important things, particularly for a church facing persecution? (See also 1:6.)

c. Why would not doing these things "quench the Spirit" (v. 19)?

4. Another way to "quench the Spirit" is to "despise prophecies" (v. 20).

   a. How should we test prophecy, and everything else?

   b. How does this instruction apply to us as we meet with other Christians in church, small groups, etc.?

## A word about 'prophecy'

What does Paul mean by prophecy? In the Old Testament, God spoke to his people through prophets. The prophets clearly understood that the words they spoke were from God because they often began by saying, "The word of the LORD..." or "This is what the LORD God says...". However, there are also strong warnings against speaking words of false prophecy, and the penalty for doing so is very harsh (e.g. Deuteronomy 13).

Jesus also warned against the dangers of being led astray by false prophets (e.g. Matt 7:15). Here in 1 Thessalonians 5:21, and also in other places in the New Testament, we are told that prophecy needs to be tested (e.g. 1 Cor 14:29; 1 John 4:1-3; 2 John 9-10). In the New Testament, it is the apostles who have the primary responsibility for proclaiming God's message of the gospel of Christ, and this is a message which can't be tampered with or undermined by anyone—even the angels (Gal 1:6-9)! However, Paul clearly thinks prophecy is a great thing, and in 1 Corinthians 14:3 and 31 he tells us that prophecy is about speaking to inform, strengthen, encourage and comfort people. And, as we've seen very clearly in 1 Thessalonians, the way in which we are to do that is by speaking to people about Jesus and the hope of the gospel.

Paul here commends prophecy and asks the Thessalonians not to despise the words of insight, instruction, encouragement and even rebuke which he has just urged them to speak (vv. 12-15). However, these words are not to be blindly accepted; they need to be tested. Their authority is only grounded in how faithfully they reflect the word of God as found in the Scriptures and the apostles' teaching. So to reject false prophecy is *not* 'quenching the Spirit'; but to refuse godly counsel—or to cease prayer and thanksgiving and to relinquish the joy of the gospel—*is* to quench the work of the Spirit among them.

5. Paul prays a final prayer for the Thessalonians in verses 23-25.

   a.  What does Paul want God to do in their lives?

   b.  How can we be confident that we will be blameless at Jesus' return?

 ## To finish

"Rejoice always, pray without ceasing, give thanks in all circumstances" (vv. 16-18). Make a list of ways you can promote joy, prayer and thanksgiving in your church.

 ## Give thanks and pray

- Thank God for the Lord Jesus Christ and for all the good things he has done, and is doing, in your life.
- Pray that he will help you to be joyful always and to hold fast to what is good.

# FOR THE LEADER

## What are Pathway Bible Guides?

The Pathway Bible Guides aim to provide simple, straightforward Bible study material for:

- Christians who are new to studying the Bible (perhaps because they've been recently converted or because they have joined a Bible study group for the first time)
- Christians who find other studies[1] too much of a stretch.

Accordingly, we've designed the studies to be short, straightforward and easy to use, with a simple vocabulary. At the same time, we've tried to do justice to the passages being studied, and to model good Bible-reading principles. We've tried to be simple without being simplistic; no-nonsense without being no-content.

The questions and answers assume a small group context, but it should be easy to adapt them to suit different situations, such as individual study and one-to-one.

## Your role as leader

Because many in your group may not be used to reading and discussing a Bible passage in a group context, a greater level of responsibility will fall to you as the leader of the discussions. There are the usual responsibilities of preparation, prayer and managing group dynamics. In addition, there will be an extra dimension of forming and encouraging good Bible reading habits in people who may not have much of an idea of what those habits look like.

Questions have been kept deliberately brief and simple. For this reason, you may have to fill in some of the gaps that may have been addressed in, say, an Interactive Bible Study. Such 'filling in' may take the form of asking follow-up questions, or using your best judgement to work out when you might need to supply background information. That sort of information, and some suggestions about other questions you could ask, may be found in the following leader's notes and in the *Genuine Imitation* CD-ROM (see page 64 for more information). In addition, a *New Bible Dictionary* is always a useful aid to preparation, and simple commentaries such as those in the *Tyndale* or *Bible Speaks Today* series are often helpful. Consult them after you have done your own preparation.

On the question of background information, these studies are written from the assumption that God's word stands alone. God works through his Holy Spirit and the leaders he has gifted—such as you—to make his meaning clear. Assuming this to be true, the best interpreter and provider of background information for Scripture will not be academic historical research, but Scripture itself. Extra historical information may be useful for the purpose of illustration, but it is unnecessary for understanding and applying what God says to us.

## The format of the studies

The discussion questions on each passage follow a simple pattern. There is a question at the beginning of each discussion that is intended to get people talking around the issues raised by the passage, and to give you some idea of how people are thinking. If the group turns out to be confident, motivated and comfortable with each other and the task at hand, you may even decide to skip this question. Alternatively, if the group members are shy or quiet, you may decide to think of related types of questions that you could add in to the study, so as to maintain momentum in a non-threatening way.

After the first question, the remaining questions work through the passage sequentially, alternating between observation, interpretation and application in a way that will become obvious when you do your own preparation. The final question of each discussion, just before the opportunity for prayer, could be used in some groups to encourage (say) one person each week to give a short talk (it could be 1 minute or 5 minutes, depending on the topic and the people). The thinking here is that there's no better way to encourage understanding of a passage than to get people to the point where they can explain it to others. Use your judgement in making the best use of this final exercise each week, depending on the people in your group.

In an average group, it should be possible to work through the study in approximately 45 minutes. But it's important that you work out what your group is capable of, given the time available, and make adjustments accordingly. Work out in advance which questions or sub-points can be omitted if time is short. And have a few supplementary questions or discussion starters up your sleeve if your group is dealing with the material quickly and hungering for more. Each group is different. It's your job as leader to use the printed material as 'Bible Guides', and not as a set of questions that you must rigidly stick to regardless of your circumstances.

## Preparation: 60/40/20

Ideally, group members should spend half an hour reading over the passage and pencilling in some answers *before* they come to the group. Not every group member will do this, of course, but encourage them with the idea that the more they prepare for the study, the more they will get out of the discussion.

In terms of your own preparation as leader, we recommend you put aside approximately *two hours*, either all at once or in two one-hour blocks, and that you divide up the time as follows:

- 60 minutes reading the passage and answering the questions yourself as best you can (without looking at the leader's notes or Bible commentaries)
- 40 minutes consulting the leader's notes (plus other resources, like commentaries). Add to your own answers, and jot down supplementary questions or other information that you want to have available as you lead the discussion. Make sure you write everything you need on the study pages—the last thing you want to do is to keep turning to the 'answers' in the back during the group discussion
- 20 minutes praying about the study and for your group members.

This 60/40/20 pattern will help you to focus on the Bible and what it's saying, rather than simply regurgitating to the group what is in the leader's notes. Remember these notes are just that—notes to offer some help and guidance. They are not the Bible! As a pattern of preparation, 60/40/20 also helps you to keep praying for yourself and your group, that God would give spiritual growth as his word is sown in your hearts (see Luke 8:4-15; 1 Cor 3:5-7).

If, for some reason, you have less or more time to spend in preparation, simply apply the 60/40/20 proportions accordingly.

---

1. Such as the Interactive Bible Study (IBS) series also available from Matthias Media.

# 1. GENUINE IMITATIONS

## 1 Thessalonians 1:1-10

▶ Remember: 60/40/20

Because the *Standing Firm* studies are designed to be brief, we have not included much background information at the beginning of the first study. If you have time to add an extra week before beginning the studies themselves, it would be a helpful exercise to read through the general background to the spread of the gospel throughout Macedonia—as found in Acts 16-17—and to track Paul's journey through this region on a map. You might also consider reading over 1 Thessalonians 2:17-3:13 to find out more about the specific background to this letter. If you then distribute these *Standing Firm* studies to people at the end of your introductory study, it will give people a week to prepare for the first *Standing Firm* study.

 ## Getting started

One of the key ideas in this study is imitation. The Thessalonians became imitators of Paul, Silvanus and Timothy, and therefore of the Lord. In turn, the Thessalonian Christians became an example to all the believers in their region. The opening question is meant to get people thinking about what makes a person someone worth imitating.

## Studying the passage

The central theme of this passage is that God changes lives. It's through the gospel that God saves people from the wrath that is to come; it's through the gospel that God changes people to be more like his son; but more than that, God uses people changed by the gospel as examples for others to imitate.

Paul knows, by the way in which the gospel message came to the Thessalonian Christians, that they are loved by God and chosen by him (question 1). The gospel came to them "not only in word, but also in power and in the Holy Spirit and with full conviction".

Many people heard the message Paul preached when he visited Thessalonica (question 2), but not everyone accepted it as the word of God because not everyone was chosen by God. Paul clearly says that accepting the word of God for what it really is, the word of God and not just the word of men (see 2:13), is only something people can do because of the powerful work of the Spirit in their lives. It is important we don't impose our own preconceived ideas of what the word coming "in power" or "in the Holy Spirit" or "with full conviction" might have meant. Rather, we should let the passage speak for itself. Verses 6-7 and 9-10 tell us that the gospel produced profound change in the lives of these people. These changes showed that they really had been deeply affected by the gospel; that their acceptance of the gospel was genuine. It was these significant changes that led Paul to the conclusion that the gospel had come to them not as mere words, but in power, in the Holy Spirit and with full conviction.

Verse 10 gives us a clear summary of the gospel message (question 3). It tells us that wrath is coming; that Jesus is God's son who died and rose again to deliver us from this wrath; and that Jesus will deliver us fully and finally when he returns from heaven.

Verses 9-10 also give us a clear summary of how we should respond to the gospel (question 4). We should turn to God; turn away from false gods; serve God; and wait for Jesus' return. In other words, faith and repentance are the proper response to the gospel.

The gospel had completely transformed the lives of these Thessalonian Christians (question 5). They no longer lived for themselves but in the service of the living and true God, and in eager expectation of Christ's return (vv. 9-10). That is, the gospel had produced a change in allegiance: they now served the living and true God. The gospel had also produce a change in their expectation about the future: they now waited for God's son from heaven. Moreover, their trust in God had transformed their deeds: their love expressed itself in persistent toil for the benefit of others; and their confidence in the eternal deliverance they had in Christ meant they were steadfast despite the very real human opposition they faced.

All of this had made them imitators of Paul, Silvanus and Timothy (question 6).

In addition, like Paul, they too had spread the gospel message in Macedonia and Achaia and the news of their faith had also "gone forth everywhere". Like Paul, their gospel words were backed up by gospel actions. Further, they had received the gospel with joy in the midst of persecution. For this also, Paul commends them as being an example.

Question 7 explores how the Thessalonians could have received the gospel with joy despite receiving it in the midst of persecution. Without the perspective of the Bible, sometimes it seems that God is at his most distant when we are in the midst of suffering or persecution. The weight of our difficulties seems to mock our trust and hope in God. Yet, when we reflect upon the cross of Christ, everything changes. Jesus' finished work and example allows us to see how the future joy of the new creation changes our present experience of afflictions, so that we can rejoice even in the midst of suffering. We are not expected to rejoice *because* of sufferings, but rather because we know that our present troubles are only a temporary experience, which God will use for our good. The joy we have springs from a deep conviction that God is in control of all things and is able to do what he has promised. It springs from the knowledge that we are following in the footsteps of our master who also suffered unjustly before entering into his glory (1 Pet 4:1; Heb 2:18). It's because of this hope that the gospel is a message worth receiving and telling (question 8; see also question 3). We face one of two possible destinies: wrath or salvation (5:9). Accepting the gospel and turning to God is the only way we find salvation. If we know this, then the only loving response is to do what the Thessalonians did and tell others also.

# 2. WALK WORTHILY

## 1 Thessalonians 2:1-12

▶ Remember: 60/40/20

 Getting started

When people say one thing and do another, we very quickly learn that they aren't worth listening to. This introductory question raises the importance of words and actions; how much of a problem it is when they don't match each other; and, as the study highlights, how powerful and positive an example it is when people's actions back up their message.

## Studying the passage

Study 1 showed how the gospel had made a huge impact on the lives of the Thessalonians. They had turned to God from idols, become imitators of Paul and the Lord, and were spreading the gospel message far and wide. But the gospel had also brought them into conflict with their fellow countrymen, and the Jews in particular (see Acts 17:1-15). In fact, as Paul points out in 2:2, he, Silvanus and Timothy had "suffered and been shamefully treated at Philippi" just before they came to Thessalonica. The first two questions in this study look at the motives behind Paul's gospel preaching. Why did Paul continue to preach such an unpopular message if it caused so much trouble? It wasn't that Paul loved conflict, or that he was trying to deceive people, or that he was stubbornly preaching a message that was clearly in error. Rather, Paul continued to preach, despite the opposition he faced, because the gospel was not his message, but God's. He couldn't change it to make it more acceptable to others because he wasn't seeking to please men. Rather, he spoke to please God, the one who had entrusted him with the task of declaring the message to others.

Because Paul was speaking God's message, he refused to use trickery or be motivated by impurity. He didn't try to butter-up his audience with words of flattery. Nor did he try to make a profit by charging people to hear the gospel. He didn't even make use of his right to financial support as an apostle of Christ (see also 1 Cor 9:4-18).

On the contrary, Paul, Silvanus and Timothy expressed their deep love for the Thessalonians by sharing not only the gospel with them, but also their own lives (question 3). They worked night and day to earn a living and so demonstrated a pattern of loving service which sought to give to others rather than be dependent on others for support. They showed loving parental concern for the Thessalonians—being gentle like a nursing mother, and encouraging and exhorting them like a father. In other words, they served the Thessalonians, putting the interests of the Thessalonians ahead of their own.

In all these ways they had demonstrated what it meant to be holy, righteous and blameless in their conduct (question 4). The reason this pattern of life is so important is that God has rescued those who trust in Christ from the wrath to come, and has called them into his own kingdom and glory (question 5). As people who seek to please God, Christians ought to base their standards of behaviour not on what is acceptable to men, but on what God desires for us. And we should do this even if it means life as a Christian is hard. God has saved us from sin, not that we might continue in it, but that we might make a fresh start and begin living a life of holiness and loving service. Paul had not only preached the gospel to the Thessalonians; he had also shown them what it meant to "walk in a manner worthy of God". And just as with Paul, it is important that our lives be consistent with the message we have accepted and which we hold out to others.

Try to leave plenty of time for question 5 and the 'To finish' application question, as this is the main opportunity for people to reflect upon the passage and how it ought to affect the way they think and act. However, make sure people clearly understand the answer to question 5 before moving on. It's important that we recognize that 'walking worthily' is only ever a *response* to salvation in Christ. We are to be holy, righteous and blameless because *we are* God's saved people; not so that we might *become* his saved people.

# 3. THE WORD AT WORK

## 1 Thessalonians 2:13-16

▶ Remember: 60/40/20

 Getting started

The gospel is a bunch of words: the message about Jesus Christ. There is a tendency for us to think that the gospel message is the place where God's work in our lives *begins*, but that God then continues to work in our lives in some other way. However, this passage affirms that God's word is the way he *continues* to work in the lives of believers. The word of the gospel is the means by which God continues to change, uphold and sustain his children, and especially so in the face of persecution.

This opening question gets people thinking about how God works in the world. Don't get sidetracked and bogged down in lengthy discussion. People may have a range of answers but it's best to move on to the rest of the study and let the passage itself make the point that God is at work through his word.

## Studying the passage

The Thessalonian Christians heard the gospel message from Paul, Silvanus and Timothy (question 1). Here in 2:13-16, Paul not only gives thanks that they heard this message, but also thanks God for the *way* in which they received it. They received it not as the word of men, but as what it really is: the word of God (question 2). Paul thanks God for this because it was not an act of mental comprehension, but spiritual recognition. Not everyone accepts the gospel for what it really is. The Jews killed the Lord Jesus and hindered Paul and his companions from speaking this saving message. The Jews did not accept this word as the word of God. So, too, others in Thessalonica opposed this new church because they had embraced the gospel. These men considered the gospel to be a dangerous and subversive message from men. But by his Spirit, God had granted to the Thessalonian Christians true spiritual insight, and they saw this word with clarity. This is why Paul thanks God. He knows that it was not his speaking that changed the Thessalonians; it was not the eloquence of his preaching or the brilliance of his answers that was the decisive factor. Rather, it was God—God's word, God's gospel, God's message of the hope of salvation.

We can't hear the gospel from the apostles—they died long ago. But we can hear the gospel message they preached as we listen to and read the Bible (question 3). The point this passage makes is that while we might read the words of Paul, John, Matthew or Luke, what we are really reading is the word of God (see also 2 Pet 1:21, 3:15-16).

Question 4 asks you to think about what Paul means when he says this word of God is "at work in you believers". Partly the answer to this comes from chapter 1, where Paul describes the tremendous change the gospel brought to the lives of the Thessalonian Christians. That is, the gospel changes our priorities, allegiance and behaviour. But also, the hope given to us by the gospel message means we can accept it with joy even in the mist of affliction (1:6). In verses 14-16 Paul describes the sort of opposition they faced. It would have been very encouraging for this Thessalonian church to know that they were not alone in suffering for the gospel, and that even the original Judean churches were facing the same trials and tribulations. But even more importantly, it was by his word and Spirit that God would keep the Thessalonians secure in Christ despite these difficulties. God's word is a living word which is at work in all believers. God works through his word and Spirit to powerfully change the lives of those who accept it. He gives them a new direction, new values, a new hope and a desire to please God. The Thessalonians needed to cling to this hope as they suffered at the hands of their opponents. They needed to remember again that the call to enter God's kingdom and glory was of greater value than any comfort in this present age. And it was the living and active word of the gospel which would remind them of what lay ahead for those who persevered until the return of the Lord.

Paul also reminds the Thessalonians of the severe consequences of rejecting this word and hindering the spread of the gospel. Some of the Jewish people were doing this, just as some Jews had also killed the prophets and the Lord himself. Some of the Thessalonian Jews had driven Paul out of that city and in so doing displeased God and opposed all mankind because they hindered the proclamation of the gospel message. These Jews did not accept that the Gentiles could be saved by the gospel.

Paul, like the other apostles and the Lord Jesus himself, was a Jew. And as we read in Acts 17:4, some of the Thessalonian Jews became Christians. So clearly Paul is not talking about *all* Jews in this passage (question 5b). Rather, he has in mind those Jews who stubbornly refuse to accept the gospel of grace he preached and who opposed it at every opportunity. The wrath that comes upon such people will fall on all who persecute God's people and hinder the spread of the gospel, Jew and Gentile alike.

It's vitally important that we recognize the word of God for what it really is (question 7). God's gospel is not one of the many sales pitches we hear each day. It's not just one truth among many. God's gospel is the only way we can truly know God, and it has authority over us. If we ignore this word, we ignore God. If we reject this word, we reject God.

##  To finish

Because God works in us by his word and Spirit, it makes sense for us to give God's word every opportunity to be at work in our lives. This will mean reading God's word, reflecting upon it, talking about it with others, being taught it by mature Christians, asking God for greater insight into the gospel and, of course, changing because of it. There are dozens of ways you can give God's word every opportunity to be at work in your life. Make sure you leave plenty of time to discuss these in your group.

# 4. GOSPEL PRIORITIES

1 Thessalonians 2:17-3:13

▶ Remember: 60/40/20

## Studying the passage

As we read in Acts 17:1-15, Paul, Silvanus and Timothy were forced to leave Thessalonica just a few weeks after their arrival. Their departure was clearly not their choice, for as Paul says in 1 Thessalonians 2:17, "we were torn away from you". So Paul made every effort to return to Thessalonica and see them "face to face". Question 1 asks you to think about why Paul was so eager to return. There are several answers you could give. He was no doubt concerned for their welfare, for he know all too well the opposition and affliction they would have been facing. He also had a deep affection for these Thessalonian Christians and considered them to be his glory and joy before the Lord (2:19-20). However, the main reason he wanted to see them face to face is so that they might be established and exhorted in their faith (3:2) and so that they might not be "moved by these afflictions" (3:3). Or, in other words, he wanted to make sure that they were standing firm in the Lord (3:8).

In 3:3-4 Paul reminds the Thessalonians that Christians are destined to suffer affliction, although he doesn't fully explain the reasons why in the passage (question 2). Some clues are given in the previous passage (2:13-18), where Paul reminds the Thessalonians that they are suffering just as the Judean churches did, and just as the Lord Jesus suffered and died. Indeed, in John 15:18-21 Jesus tells his disciples that "A servant is not greater than his master. If they persecuted me, they will also persecute you". Rather than being something surprising, suffering in this life is the expected consequence of following Jesus.

Having been sent to establish and exhort the Thessalonians, Timothy has returned with the good news of their faith and love (question 3). While Paul might be suffering "distress and affliction" (3:7), this report brings him comfort and joy. Note that Paul is not focused on his own needs—his concern is that the Thessalonians be built in their faith.

Question 4 asks you to look at Paul's prayer in verses 11-13. Love is a deep concern for others—doing what's best for them ahead of our own interests (question 4a). We see loving concern perfectly demonstrated in the gospel of the crucified Christ. We also see it in the way Paul cared for the Thessalonian church. He was not content to simply preach the gospel; he sought to encourage, support and strengthen those under his care. He was even willing to put himself in danger so that he might help these new converts. Love not only reflects the character of God; it's the pathway to holiness. Paul prays that the Thessalonians would abound in love *so that* they might be established blameless in holiness. If we want to be holy, we must abound in love.

Holiness is about being perfectly pure and carries with it the idea of being distinct or set apart (question 4b). God calls on his people to be holy just as he is holy (e.g. 1 Pet 1:15; Lev 11:44). Holiness is important because without it we will not see the holy God (Heb 12:14), and we see this idea clearly reflected in this passage. We will stand before God at the coming of the Lord Jesus, but we will only do so having been established "blameless in holiness" (3:13).

Question 5 asks the group to think back to the goals they wrote down in the 'Getting started' question. The apostle Paul knew that there was nothing more important than standing firm in Christ. And as we have seen, standing firm did not mean standing still, but abounding in love and being established blameless in holiness. Question 6 flows on from this, because if we embrace the gospel priorities of love and holiness then we need to be clear on how we can progress in these. Clearly Paul expected the Thessalonians to make every effort to be found holy on that last day. And he spends some time reminding them of his loving example so that they might imitate it more and more. But at the same time we must remember that 3:11-13 is a prayer. Paul is asking that *God* would make them more loving, and that *God* would establish their hearts blameless in holiness. *God* will complete in us the work of salvation made possible through Christ's death on our behalf. However, God chooses to bring this about through our own self-discipline, perseverance and effort. He will strengthen us for the task by his word and Spirit. Yet, because of our own weakness, we will sometimes fail. We must toil and persevere at holiness, while reflecting upon the love of God expressed in the cross and in prayerful dependence upon him.

# 5. GOD'S WILL, YOUR SANCTIFICATION

## 1 Thessalonians 4:1-12

▶ Remember: 60/40/20

 Getting started

The introductory question is designed to get the group thinking about their words and actions. Christians should be backing up their words with actions. At the same time, Christians don't claim to be perfect, although we ought to work hard to be holy and blameless.

## Studying the passage

The Thessalonian Christians already know how they ought to live and to please God—in fact they are already doing this. Paul wants them to "do so more and more" (question 1). Paul puts this another way in verse 3 when he says, "this is the will of God, your sanctification" (question 2a). Question 2b then goes on to explore what this means. In Greek, the words for holiness and sanctification are almost identical. So Paul is simply emphasizing what he said back in 3:13 where he prayed that God would establish their hearts blameless in holiness. This will mean all sorts of things in practice, some of which you will have discussed in the previous study.

Paul goes on to talk about two specific areas in which the Thessalonians are to live holy lives: in sexual purity (questions 3 to 5), and in brotherly love (questions 6 and 7).

Christians are to abstain from sexual immorality. The Bible doesn't define sexual immorality by making a big list of activities to avoid. Rather, we are told that the proper place for sexual expression is in a lifelong union between a man and a women (i.e. marriage). Everything else is to be avoided.[1] Being ignorant of God, the Gentiles are directed by the "passion of lust". Christians however, are to exercise self-control so that they behave in holiness and honour. The difference between these two is service. Lust is self-serving and ultimately destructive. Holy and honourable behaviour seeks the good of other people. In marriage, this will mean using our bodies to satisfy the needs of our marriage partner and no-one else. For the unmarried it means abstaining from sex, because this is pleasing to God and loving towards others.

To behave in a sexually immoral way is therefore not only unloving, but also rebellious. The person who wrongs their brother in this matter (presumably by engaging in inappropriate sexual behaviour with them or with their marriage partner) will be brought to justice by God. God has called Christians not in impurity but in holiness. To disregard this instruction is therefore a very serious matter.

Paul wants the Thessalonians to abound more and more in brotherly love. Christians ought to have a deep concern for others, and, like all true love, this brotherly love is expressed in actions. Paul is asking and urging them to continue in the pattern of loving service they were already demonstrating. As we read in 1:3, their love was shown by their labour. In 4:9-10, Paul commends them for their acts of service throughout Macedonia. While they might have been tempted to retaliate against those persecuting them, Paul encourages them to live quietly and mind their own affairs. This kind of quiet and peaceable life is loving because it seeks the good of others rather than our own desire for revenge. Moreover, they are to follow Paul's example of hard work (2:9) so that they also might be a burden on no-one. Because the nature of love is giving to others—not taking from them—one clear application of this principle of love is to work—to work in order to not be a burden on others and also to have something to share with those who are in genuine need. Paul also wants them to work so that they might "live properly before outsiders"—or, more literally, "so that you may *walk* properly before outsiders". They are to walk in a manner worthy of the gospel so as to make the gospel message attractive, not bring it into disrepute. This theme is picked up in question 8 which explores how walking in love is not only a demonstration of the holiness to which we are called, but also a demonstration of the power of the gospel to change lives. Our gospel-produced actions should adorn the gospel message itself.

---

1. For a full discussion of this topic see chapter 9 of Michael Hill's book: *The How and Why of Love*, Matthias Media, Sydney, 2002.

# 6. HOPE IN THE LORD

## 1 Thessalonians 4:13-18

▶ Remember: 60/40/20

## Studying the passage

In verse 14 we are told that God will bring with Jesus those who have fallen asleep. In verses 16-17, it is the dead in Christ who rise and are then caught up with him. Clearly, Paul is using the word "asleep" to speak of people who have died, and this is confirmed by the fact Paul expects this teaching to change the way Christians grieve (question 1). He wants them to be informed because he does not want them to grieve "as others do who have no hope" (question 2). We should note that Paul is not saying that he does not want them to grieve at all, but that he doesn't want them to grieve in the same way as those who have no hope. Clearly, Paul expects the Christian hope to change our grief in a significant way.

The Christian hope is given by Paul in verse 14 (question 3): "For since we believe that Jesus died and rose again, even so, through Jesus, God will bring with him those who have fallen asleep". There is a simple 'if... then' logic to the Christian hope. If Jesus has died, and if he has risen from the dead, then we can be absolutely sure that God will also raise our Christian brothers and sisters who have died. Jesus has done two things: firstly, he has died; secondly, he has risen again from the dead. In contrast, those who have fallen asleep have done only one thing: they have died. Paul's clear expectation is that those who have died in Christ will certainly also experience this second thing—that is, resurrection to new life.

It is because Jesus' death and resurrection are objective historical facts that the Christian hope is a sure and certain reality, rather than just wishful thinking (question 4). We don't believe in something that is impossible, but in something that has already happened to Jesus and which we too will also experience.

Paul tells the Thessalonians that the dead in Christ will rise first when Jesus returns. They won't miss out on anything because they will precede those who are still alive (question 5).

The Lord's return is described as being announced by a "cry of command, with the voice of an archangel, and with the sound of the trumpet of God". Clearly, the emphasis is on this event being proclaimed so loudly that no-one will be able to misunderstand what is happening. No-one will fail to recognize the triumphant return of the king (question 6). The purpose of the Lord's return is to bring all his people, those who are asleep and those who are alive, to be with him forever (question 7). We aren't given any details of what this new resurrection life will be like. The focus is on who we are with: the Lord Jesus.

The Christian hope has profound implications for our understanding of death and therefore our grief (question 8). Death is not the end, and Christian brothers and sisters who die will be raised again at the Lord's return. This means we have words of encouragement with which to comfort those who grieve. The death and resurrection of Christ removes the sting of death and gives us hope and joy.

In this study the topic of the 'rapture' might be raised. The word "rapture" is derived from the Latin equivalent of the Greek term for 'caught up'—the snatching away of believers (4:17). The Bible has very little to say about this snatching away, or rapture, and the only other passages which perhaps discuss this issue are Matthew 24 and Luke 17, where some people are taken and others are left. Given the various positions people hold concerning the millennium, the tribulation and the rapture, there is no shortage of differing views on the order and significance of these events. The most natural reading of 1 Thessalonians would seem to suggest that Paul anticipates a single climactic return in which the Lord gathers his people to himself to be with him forever.

Don't get sidetracked by these issues, and it would be unhelpful for you as the leader to raise them in your group. If this is a topic which is of particular interest to some members of your group then it might be best to talk through the relevant Bible passages with them at some other time. Rather, during the study, focus on the hope we have and how we can be putting Paul's advice into practice (i.e. "encourage one another with these words").

# 7. READY FOR HIS RETURN

## 1 Thessalonians 5:1-11

▶ Remember: 60/40/20

 Getting started

When we have a big event coming up, we make plans; we get ourselves ready for the event. This question is simply to prompt people to see that in everyday life, we know that we need to plan for significant occasions. The rest of the study will go on to explore how this should be especially the case as we make ourselves ready for the return of Jesus.

## Studying the passage

The topic of the Lord's return has been raised several times in this letter: the Thessalonians turned to God from idols to serve the living and true God, and to wait for his son from heaven (1:9-10); Paul prays that the Lord would establish the Thessalonians' hearts blameless in holiness before God at the coming of the Lord Jesus with all his saints (3:13); and Paul tells them more about the return of the Lord and the resurrection of the dead in the previous section of the letter (4:13-18).

For people whose hope was bound up with this day—for people who wait and long for this day in the midst of persecution—the natural question is, "When? When will this day arrive?" Paul tells them that the day of the Lord will come "like a thief in the night" (question 1). Thieves, if they're any good at what they do, come unexpectedly and try to catch people by surprise. So too, the day of the Lord will come when people least expect it. At the very time when "people are saying, 'there is peace and security', then sudden destruction will come upon them" (v. 3). However, Christians should not be surprised by this day (question 2). The reason for this is given in verses 4-5: we are children of the light and of the day. This imagery of light and darkness is particularly appropriate given the topic Paul is addressing. Firstly, thieves often strike under the cover of darkness. Secondly, the Thessalonians have knowledge concerning the Lord's return (v. 2). They are fully aware of Paul's teaching on this topic. In this sense they are not in the dark about the Lord's return. Finally, they are to be God's holy people, and so their deeds are to be the good deeds appropriate to the children of light, not the evil deeds of the children of darkness. In other words, the Thessalonians will be fully prepared for the Lord's return—whenever it comes—by their knowledge, godliness and hope in the salvation Christ brings.

Questions 3-5 go on to explore in more detail how we can be ready for the Lord's return. As children of the light we are not to sleep but be "awake and sober" (v. 6). The way to be awake and sober is to "put on the breastplate of faith and love, and for a helmet the hope of salvation" (v. 8). In other words, Christians ought to arm themselves with faith, love and hope. We know the Lord will return to judge those who do evil; we know that Jesus' death and resurrection is the means by which we can be saved from this judgement; we know there is no future in a life characterized by the deeds of darkness; and so we should live as holy and blameless people. These are the things we should be encouraging and fostering in our lives and in the lives of our fellow believers.

Sleep: In the previous passage Paul has used the word "asleep" to mean those who have died safe in the Lord's keeping. In 5:6-7 the word is used differently, in the context of the way of life appropriate to children of the day and of the light. In this context, Paul calls on the children of the day to be awake and sober, in contrast to the activities which characterize the night—sleep and drink. The call to be awake and sober is the call to be alert, prepared and waiting, particularly in light of the warning that a thief is coming. We see this same idea in passages such as Matthew 24:36-51, where Jesus warns his disciples to be ready so that he will find them doing his will.

However in 1 Thessalonians 5:10, Paul reverts back to using the words "awake" and "asleep" in the same way as he did in 4:13-18—that is, to mean those who are alive at the Lord's return and those who have died in Christ prior to his return. The destiny of all Christians is to live with the Lord, so it doesn't matter whether we are alive or have died prior to his coming. We will all live with him forever because we are destined for salvation, not wrath. Clearly, in verse 10, Paul cannot be saying that because of Jesus' death it doesn't matter whether we act as children of light or children of darkness. The context makes Paul's point clear, so it's perfectly natural for Paul to revert to using "asleep" and "awake" in the same sense that he used them in the previous passage.

Verses 9-10 are also noteworthy because they give us a very clear explanation of the significance of Jesus' death and resurrection (questions 5a and 5b): specifically, that Jesus' death was penal (i.e. his death paid the penalty necessary to avert judgement and bring peace and salvation; he died to save us from God's anger) and substitutionary (i.e. Jesus died "for us", in our place, instead of us). Jesus was able to do this because as a man he could stand in our place, and as the son of God his death was enough to pay for the sins of every person. Other passages to which you could refer include Romans 3:21-26, 5:6-11; Titus 2:11-14; Hebrews 7:26-28, 9:11-15, 9:27-28.

# 8. A GOSPEL CHURCH AT WORK

......................................................................

## 1 Thessalonians 5:12-28

▶ Remember: 60/40/20

 **Getting started**

This question gives people the chance to express their ideas freely about church. The study itself will then challenge people with Paul's view of healthy church life.

## Studying the passage

The common theme in the seemingly unrelated set of instructions in verses 12-28 is 'church': specifically, what healthy church life will look like. Paul calls on the church to recognize, respect and esteem those who labour and work for the benefit of the church (question 1a). These people are servants of the church, guiding, loving and even admonishing others where necessary. And because of their loving service, they are to be highly esteemed in love (question 1b). Their service is not to be resisted or opposed, because they are doing their work not for their own sake, but for the benefit of others.

While the church is to recognize these leaders, every member of the church is to participate in the work of encouraging and building the church (question 2). Everyone is called upon to admonish the idle, encourage the fainthearted and help the weak. Paul has previously instructed people to work and support themselves, warning them against being dependent on others. But rather than only the leaders being those who warn others, here the whole church is to take responsibility for warning people against the dangers of idleness. This might be a painful and difficult task, but it is a necessary one. Likewise, the whole church is to encourage those who are fainthearted. There are always people who find the going tough, who become discouraged. And particularly in the face of persecution, there will be people who begin to contemplate giving it all up. They need comfort and encouragement, and this is a task that every church member can and ought to participate in. Likewise, the weak—whether spiritually or physically weak—need help and support. They might need some practical care, or someone to talk to about their struggles. Whatever it is, this is the sort of loving care that every member of the church can provide. Finally, those who are part of the church are to be patient with everyone. It is easy for bitterness or impatience to creep into our relationships, especially when we are continually trying to help those in need. Paul urges Christians to be patient with one another, not expecting change in others to be rapid or our support to be a short term offer. Some people will need help for a long time.

Paul wants to see a church in which people are intimately involved with one another while also being at peace (question 2i). Sometimes the more we get to know people, the more conflict emerges. But Paul expects the gospel of grace and forgiveness to set the tone for the relationships amongst the Thessalonian Christians. They are not to repay evil with evil, but to always seek the best for others, just as God did for us in Christ Jesus.

Paul wants to see churches which are in step with the Spirit (questions 3 and 4). The Spirit had renewed the hearts and minds of the Thessalonians so they could receive the gospel as it really is—the word of God. Moreover, they received this gospel with the joy of the Holy Spirit. Paul wants them to continue in this way and not to quench the Spirit by departing from genuine gospel teaching, or failing to be joyous and thankful in response to the gospel. As such, they are to keep praying and rejoicing and thanking God for what they have received. And they are to test prophecy to make sure it conforms to the gospel they received. If it doesn't, they are to reject it. However, if what is spoken is true to Scripture then they are certainly not to despise this wise counsel, for they should take hold of everything good and hold fast to it. Prophecy can be a contentious issue, but the extra material included in the study on 'prophecy' should set your group on the right track.

Finally, Paul reiterates his great desire for the Thessalonians (question 5). He wants God, who is faithful, to complete in them the work already begun. He wants God to sanctify them completely so that their whole being is kept blameless for the coming of the Lord Jesus. And Paul knows that the God who has faithfully cared for this church despite Paul's forced absence, will surely bring them to that final day, blameless in holiness.

Matthias Media is an evangelical publishing ministry that seeks to persuade all Christians of the truth of God's purposes in Jesus Christ as revealed in the Bible, and equip them with high-quality resources, so that by the work of the Holy Spirit they will:

- abandon their lives to the honour and service of Christ in daily holiness and decision-making
- pray constantly in Christ's name for the fruitfulness and growth of his gospel
- speak the Bible's life-changing word whenever and however they can—in the home, in the world and in the fellowship of his people.

It was in 1988 that we first started pursuing this mission, and in God's kindness we now have more than 300 different ministry resources being used all over the world. These resources range from Bible studies and books through to training courses and audio sermons.

To find out more about our large range of very useful resources, and to access samples and free downloads, visit our website:

## www.matthiasmedia.com

## How to buy our resources

1. Direct from us over the internet:
   - in the US: www.matthiasmedia.com
   - in Australia and the rest of the world: www.matthiasmedia.com.au

> Register at our website for our **free** regular email update to receive information about the latest new resources, **exclusive special offers**, and free articles to help you grow in your Christian life and ministry.

2. Direct from us by phone: please visit our website for current phone contact information.

3. Through a range of outlets in various parts of the world. Visit **www.matthiasmedia.com/contact** for details about recommended retailers in your part of the world, including www.thegoodbook.co.uk in the United Kingdom.

4. Trade enquiries can be addressed to:
   - in the US and Canada: sales@matthiasmedia.com
   - in Australia and the rest of the world: sales@matthiasmedia.com.au

5. Visit **GoThereFor.com** for subscription-based access to a great-value range of digital resources.

# Pathway Bible Guides

Pathway Bible Guides are simple, straightforward easy-to-read Bible studies, ideal for groups who are new to studying the Bible, or groups with limited time for study.We've designed the studies to be short and easy to use, with an uncomplicated vocabulary. At the same time, we've tried to do justice to the passages being studied, and to model good Bible-reading principles. Pathway Bible Guides are simple without being simplistic; no-nonsense without being no-content.

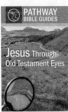

FOR MORE INFORMATION OR TO ORDER CONTACT:

Matthias Media
Email: sales@matthiasmedia.com.au
www.matthiasmedia.com.au

Matthias Media (USA)
Email: sales@matthiasmedia.com
www.matthiasmedia.com